MW00914704

GROWING IN THE GOSPEL

What Does Jesus Genealogy In Matthew's Gospel Tell Us?

An Hebraic Analysis of Matthew 1:1-17
using Ancient Bible Study Methods

Michael Harvey Koplitz

All Scripture quotations, unless otherwise noted, are taken from the *New American Standard Bible*®, Copyright © 1960, 1962, 1963, 1968, 1971, 1972, 1973, 1975, 1977, 1995 by the Lockman Foundation. Used by permission (www.Lockman.org)

The NASB uses italic to indicate words that have been added for clarification. Citations are shown with large capital letters.

Published by Michael H. Koplitz

ISBN-13: 978-1722240240

ISBN-10: 1722240245

Table of Contents

Introduction

I have been told by congregation members that the genealogy of Jesus found in Matthew and Mark are just boring. Who wants to read a long list of names that are difficult to pronounce? It is my hope that when you examine this book that you will change your mind about the genealogy and other ones that you find in the Scripture.

There are hidden treasures of information that our God has placed in every passage of Scripture especially the genealogy of Jesus Christ in Matthew's Gospel. By learning the Ancient Bible Study methods that are taught at http://bibleinteract.tv you will learn how to ask questions about the Scripture and you will learn that there is a lot of treasures to be discovered in the Scripture. The LORD had the books of the Bible written in such a way that numerous explanations can arise.

If you are unfamiliar with Ancient Bible Study methods you will want to read the next two chapters. You can also come to our website and watch some videos on this method of biblical interpretation.

The main differences between the Greek method and Hebraic method of teaching

Once you are aware of the two teaching styles, you will be able to determine if you are in a class or reading a book, whether the analysis and/or teaching method is either in a Greek or Hebraic method. In the Greek method it is automatically thought that the instructor is right because of advanced knowledge. In the college situation, it is because the professor has his/her Ph.D. in some area of study, so one assumes that he or she knows everything about the topic. For example, Rodney Dangerfield played the role of a middle-aged man going to college. His English midterm was to write about Kurt Vonnegut Jr. Since he didn't understand any of Vonnegut's books he hired Vonnegut himself to the write the midterm. When it was returned to him, the English Professor told Dangerfield that whoever wrote the paper knew nothing about Vonnegut. This is an example of the Greek method of teaching. Did the Ph.D. English professor think that she knew more about Vonnegut's writings than Vonnegut did? [1]

In the Greek teaching method, the professor or the instructor claims to be the authority. If you are attending a Bible study class and the class leader says, "I will teach you the only way to understand this biblical book," you may want to consider the implications. This method is common since most Seminaries and Bible colleges teach a Greek method of learning, which is the same method the church has been utilizing for centuries.

Hebraic teaching methods are different. The teacher wants the students to challenge what they hear. It is through questioning that a student can learn. In

---

[1] *Back to School*. Performed by Rodney Dangerfield. Hollywood: CA: Paper Clip Productions, 1986. DVD.

addition, the teacher wants his/her students to excel to a point where the student becomes the teacher.

It is said that if two rabbis come together to discuss a passage of Scripture, the result will be at least ten different opinions. All points of view are acceptable if biblical evidence can support the points. It is permissible and encouraged for students to have multiple opinions. There is a depth to God's Word, and God wants us to find all His messages that are placed in the Scriptures.

Seeking out the meaning of the Scriptures beyond the literal meaning is essential to fully understanding God's Word.[2] The Greek method of learning the Scriptures has prevailed over the centuries. One problem is that only the literal interpretation of Scripture was often

---

[2] Davis, Anne Kimball. *The Synoptic Gospels*. MP3. Albuquerque: NM: BibleInteract, 2012.

viewed as valid, as prompted by Martin Luther's "sola literalis" meaning that only the literal interpretation of Scripture was valid. The Fundamentalist movements of today are generally based on the literal interpretation of the Scripture. Therefore, they do not believe that God placed any deeper, hidden, or secret meanings in the Word.

The students of the Scriptures who learn through Hebraic training and understanding have drawn a different conclusion. The Hebrew language itself leads to different possible interpretations because of the construction of the language. The Hebraic method of Bible study opens avenues of thought about God's revelations in the Scripture that may have never been considered. A question may be raised about the Scripture being studied for which there may not be an immediate answer. If so, it becomes the responsibility of the learners to uncover the meaning. Also, remember that multiple opinions about the meaning of Scripture are also acceptable if Scripture can support them.

Methodology

The methodology employed is to use First Century Scripture study methods integrated with the customs and culture of Yeshua's day to examine the Hebrew and Christian Scriptures, thus gathering a deeper understanding by learning the Scriptures in the way the people of Yeshua's day did.

The Process of Discovery

I have titled the methodology of analyzing a passage of Scripture in a Hebraic manner the "Process of Discovery." This methodology was developed by the author bringing together the various areas of linguistic and cultural understanding. There are several sections to the process and not all the sections apply to every passage of Scripture. The overall result of developing this process is to give the reader a framework into the ideas being presented.

The "Process of Discovery" starts with a Scripture passage. If the passage is in a poetic form, it is identified. Possible poetic techniques include: parallelism, chiastic structures, and repetition. Formatting the passage in its poetic form allows the reader to be able to visualize what the first century CE listener was hearing. The chiasms are labeled by their corresponding sections, for example: A, B, C, B', A'. Not all passages of the Scriptures have a poetic form.

The next step is to "question the narrative," which is accomplished by assuming the reader knows nothing about the passage. Therefore, the questions go from the simple to the complex. The next task is to identify any linguistic patterns. Linguistic patterns include, but are not limited to: irony, simile, metaphor, symbolism, idioms, hyperbole, figurative language, personification, and allegory.

Any translation inconsistencies discovered between the English NASB version and either the Hebrew or Greek versions are identified. There are times when a Hebrew or Greek word can be translated in more than one way. Inconsistencies also can be created by the translation committee, which may have decided to use traditional language instead of the actual translation. The decision of the translation committee can be generally found in the Preface or Introduction to the Bible. Perhaps some of the inconsistencies were intentionally added to convey some deeper meaning therefore, the inconsistencies need to be examined.

Echoes of the Hebrew Scriptures in the Christian Scripture are identified. This occurs when a passage from the Hebrew Scripture is used in the Christian

Scripture or when a command is directly discussed in the Christian Scriptures. [3] In addition, echoes can be found when Torah (Genesis through Deuteronomy) passages are used in other Hebrew Bible books. In addition to echoes, cross references are listed. A cross reference is a reference to another verse in the Scripture which can assist the reader to understand the verse that is being read.

The names of persons mentioned in the passage are listed. Many of the Hebrew names have meaning and may be associated with places or actions. Jewish parents used to name their children based on what they felt God had in store for their child. An example of this is Abraham whose original name was Abram and was changed to mean eternal father (in this case Abram's name was changed by God to Abraham indicating a

---

[3] Mitzvot are the 613 commandments found in the Torah that please God. There are positive and negative commandments. The list was first development by Maimonides. The full list can be found at: ttp://www.jewfaq.org/613.htm.

function he was to perform). When the Hebrew Bible gives names, many of the occurrences will indicate something special to the reader/listener. The same importance can hold true for the names of places. The time it takes to travel between places can supply insight to the event.

Key words are identified in a verse when they are important to an understanding of that passage. There are no rules for selecting the key words. Searching for other occurrences of the keywords in Scripture in a concordance is necessary to understand how the word was being used; this must be done in either Hebrew or Greek, not in English. A classic Hebraic approach is to find the usage of a word in the Scripture by finding other verses that contain the word. The usage of a word, in its original language, is discovered by searching the Scripture in the language of the word. The verses that contain the word being researched are identified and a pattern for the usage of the word is discerned. Each verse is examined to see what the usage of the word is which, may reveal a pattern for the word's usage. For Hebrew words the first usage of the word in the Scripture, especially if used in the Torah, is important. For the Greek words the Christian Scriptures are used to determine the word usage in the Scripture. Sometimes finding the equivalent Greek word in the Septuagint then analyzing its usage in Hebrew can be very helpful.

The Rules of Hillel for Bible understanding can be used when applicable. Hillel was a Torah scholar who lived shortly before Yeshua's day. Hillel developed several rules for Torah students to interpret the Scriptures which are referred to as halachic midrash. In several cases these rules are helpful in the analysis of the Scripture.

After the linguistic analysis is complete an examination of the cultural implications will be examined. The culture is important because it is not specifically referenced in the biblical narratives as indicated earlier.

From the linguistic analysis and the cultural understanding, it is possible to obtain a deeper meaning of the Scripture beyond the literal meaning of the plain text. That is what the listeners of Yeshua's time were doing. They put the linguistics and the culture together without even having to contemplate it. They simply did it.

This will lead to a conclusion or a set of conclusions about what the passage is talking about. Most of the time the Hebraic analysis leads to the desire for a deeper analysis to fully understand what Yeshua was talking about or what was happening to Him. Whatever the result, a new deeper understanding of the Scripture will be obtained.

The components of the Process of Discovery are:

Linguistics Section

Linguistic Structure of the Scripture

Discussion

Questioning the Passage[4]

Verse Comparison on citations or proof text

Translation inconsistencies

Biblical Personalities

---

[4] (Answers to these questions are offered for discussion purposes and you may have different answers. Remember, answers must be defendable from Scripture. In addition, you may have additional questions about the passage that is not covered. This applies to this section and to the Questioning the Passage in the Cultural section.)

Biblical Locations

Phrase Study

Scripture cross references

Echoes

Rules of Hillel

Culture Section

Discussion

Questioning the passage culturally

Culture and Linguistics Section

Discussion

Main/Center Point

Only the applicable sections are in this document.

Abbreviations

Bibleworks V10[5] was used for the Scriptures used in this study guide. Below are the abbreviations used in the software.

Pentateuch	GEN	EXO	LEV	NUM	DEU
Historical & Poetic	JOS 1KI NEH ECC	JDG 2KI EST SOL	RUT 1CH JOB	1SA 2CH PSA	2SA EZR PRO
Prophets	ISA HOS MIC ZEC	JER JOE NAH MAL	LAM AMO HAB	EZE OBA ZEP	DAN JON HAG

---

[5] "Bible Version Abbreviations." Abbreviations. N.p., n.d. Web. 29 Oct. 2016.

Gospels	MAT	MAR	LUK	JOH	ACT
Paul	ROM PHI 2TI	1COCO L TIT	2CO 1TH PHM	GAL 2TH	EPH 1TI
Apostles	HEB 2JO	JAM 3JO	1PE JUD	2PE REV	1JO
Apocrypha	1ES 3MA PSS PRA JDT 4MA	BAR PRM TOB ODE EPJ PSX	1MA WIS SUS 4ES 2MA SIP	SIR BELLA O ESG JSA JDA	TBS SUT DAT BET DNG

The following is a list of aliases for BibleWorks book name abbreviations. See the <u>Book Names</u> section of the Options window for details on how to add to or change these aliases.

Internal	Name used i	Name used	Alias 1	Alias 2

Name	n Browse Window	in Exported Verse Lists		
Gen	Genesis	Gen.	Gen	Genesis
Exo	Exodus	Exod.	Exo	Exodus
Lev	Leviticus	Lev.	Lev	Leviticus
Num	Numbers	Num.	Num	Numbers
Deu	Deuteronomy	Deut.	Deu	Deuteronomy
Jos	Joshua	Jos.	Jos	Joshua
Jdg	Judges	Jdg.	Jdg	Judges
Rut	Ruth	Ruth	Rut	Ruth
1Sa	1 Samuel	1 Sam.	1Sa	1Samuel
2Sa	2 Samuel	2 Sam.	2Sa	2Samuel
1Ki	1 Kings	1 Ki.	1Ki	1Kings
2Ki	2 Kings	2 Ki.	2Ki	2Kings
1Ch	1 Chronicles	1 Chr.	1Ch	1Chronicles
2Ch	2 Chronicle	2 Chr.	2Ch	2 Chronicles

	s			
Ezr	Ezra	Ezr.	Ezr	Ezra
Neh	Nehemiah	Neh.	Neh	Nehemiah
Est	Esther	Est.	Est	Esther
Job	Job	Job	Job	Job
Psa	Psalm	Ps.	Psa	Psalm
Pro	Proverbs	Prov.	Pro	Proverbs
Ecc	Ecclesiastes	Eccl.	Ecc	Ecclesiastes
Sol	Song of Solomon	Cant.	Sol	Song
Isa	Isaiah	Isa.	Isa	Isaiah
Jer	Jeremiah	Jer.	Jer	Jeremiah
Lam	Lamentations	Lam.	Lam	Lamentations
Eze	Ezekiel	Ezek.	Eze	Ezekiel
Dan	Daniel	Dan.	Dan	Daniel
Hos	Hosea	Hos.	Hos	Hosea
Joe	Joel	Joel	Joe	Joel
Amo	Amos	Amos	Amo	Amos
Oba	Obadiah	Obad.	Ob	Obadiah

			a	
Jon	Jonah	Jon.	Jon	Jonah
Mic	Micah	Mic.	Mic	Micah
Nah	Nahum	Nah.	Nah	Nahum
Hab	Habakkuk	Hab.	Hab	Habakkuk
Zep	Zephaniah	Zeph.	Zep	Zephaniah
Hag	Haggai	Hag.	Hag	Haggai
Zec	Zechariah	Zech.	Zec	Zechariah
Mal	Malachi	Mal.	Mal	Malachi
Mat	Matthew	Matt.	Mat	Matthew
Mar	Mark	Mk.	Mar	Mark
Luk	Luke	Lk.	Luk	Luke
Joh	John	Jn.	Joh	John
Act	Acts	Acts	Act	Acts
Rom	Romans	Rom.	Rom	Romans
1Co	1 Corinthians	1 Co.	1Co	1Corinthians
2Co	2	2 Co.	2C	2Corinthia

	Corinthia ns		o	ns
Gal	Galatians	Gal.	Gal	Galatians
Eph	Ephesians	Eph.	Eph	Ephesians
Phi	Philippian s	Phil.	Phi	Philippians
Col	Colossian s	Col.	Col	Colossians
1Th	1 Thessalon ians	1 Thess.	1Th	1Thessalon ians
2Th	2 Thessalon ians	2 Thess.	2Th	2Thessalon ians
1Ti	1 Timothy	1 Tim.	1Ti	1Timothy
2Ti	2 Timothy	2 Tim.	2Ti	2Timothy
Tit	Titus	Tit.	Tit	Titus
Phm	Philemon	Phlm.	Phm	Philemon
Heb	Hebrews	Heb.	Heb	Hebrews
Jam	James	Jas.	Jam	James
1Pe	1 Peter	1 Pet.	1Pe	1Peter
2Pe	2 Peter	2 Pet.	2Pe	2Peter
1Jo	1 John	1 Jn.	1Jo	1John

2Jo	2 John	2 Jn.	2Jo	2John
3Jo	3 John	3 Jn.	3Jo	3John
Jud	Jude	Jude	Jud	Jude
Rev	Revelation	Rev.	Rev	Revelation
1Es	1 Esdras	1 Es.	1Es	1Esdras
Jdt	Judith	Jdt.	Jdt	Judith
Tob	Tobit	Tob.	Tob	Tobit
1Ma	1 Maccabees	1 Ma.	1Ma	1Maccabees
2Ma	2 Maccabees	2 Ma.	2Ma	2Maccabees
3Ma	3 Maccabees	3 Ma.	3Ma	3Maccabees
4Ma	4 Maccabees	4 ma.	4Ma	4Maccabees
Ode	Odes	Odes	Ode	Odes
Wis	Wisdom	Wis.	Wis	Wisdom
Sir	Sirach	Sir.	Sir	Sirach
Sip	Sip	Sip	Sip	Sip

Pss	Psalms of Solomon	Ps. Sol.	Pss	
Bar	Baruch	Bar.	Bar	Baruch
Epj	Epistle of Jeremiah	Ep. Jer.	Epj	
Sus	Susanna	Sus.	Sus	Susanna
Bel	Bel	Bel.	Bel	Bel
Pra	Prayer of Azariah	Pr. Az.	Pra	Azariah
Dng	Daniel (Greek)	Dng	Dng	Dng
Prm	Prayer of Manasseh	Pr. Man.	Prm	Manasseh
Psx	Psalm(151)	Psx.	Psx	
Lao	Laodiceans	Lao.	Lao	Laodiceans
4Es	4 Esdras	4 Es.	4Es	4Esdras
Esg	Esther (Greek)	Esg.	Esg	
Jsa	Joshua (A)	Jsa.	Jsa	
Jda	Judges (A)	Jda.	Jda	
Tbs	Tobit (S)	Tbs.	Tbs	
Sut	Susanna (TH)	Sut.	Sut	

Dat	Daniel (TH)	Dat.	Dat	
Bet	Bel (TH)	Bet.	Bet	
WCF	WCF	WCF	WCF	
WLC	WLC	WLC	WLC	
WSC	WSC	WSC	WSC	

Hebraic Analysis of Matthew 1:1-17

Language

New American Standard 1995	Koine Greek
[1] The record of the genealogy of Jesus the Messiah, the son of David, the son of Abraham: [2] Abraham was the father of Isaac, Isaac the father of Jacob, and Jacob the father of Judah and his brothers. [3] Judah was the father of Perez and Zerah by Tamar, Perez was the father of Hezron, and Hezron the father of Ram. [4] Ram was the father of Amminadab, Amminadab the father of Nahshon, and Nahshon	Βίβλος γενέσεως Ἰησοῦ χριστοῦ, υἱοῦ Δαυίδ, υἱοῦ Ἀβραάμ. [2] Ἀβραὰμ ἐγέννησεν τὸν Ἰσαάκ· Ἰσαὰκ δὲ ἐγέννησεν τὸν Ἰακώβ· Ἰακὼβ δὲ ἐγέννησεν τὸν Ἰούδαν καὶ τοὺς ἀδελφοὺς αὐτοῦ· [3] Ἰούδας δὲ ἐγέννησεν τὸν Φαρὲς καὶ τὸν Ζαρὰ ἐκ τῆς Θάμαρ· Φαρὲς δὲ ἐγέννησεν τὸν Ἐσρώμ· Ἐσρὼμ δὲ ἐγέννησεν τὸν Ἀράμ· [4] Ἀρὰμ δὲ ἐγέννησεν τὸν Ἀμιναδάβ· Ἀμιναδὰβ δὲ ἐγέννησεν τὸν Ναασσών· Ναασσὼν δὲ ἐγέννησεν τὸν Σαλμών·

the father of Salmon.

⁵ Salmon was the father of Boaz by Rahab, Boaz was the father of Obed by Ruth, and Obed the father of Jesse.

⁶ Jesse was the father of David the king. David was the father of Solomon by Bathsheba who had been the wife of Uriah.

⁷ Solomon was the father of Rehoboam, Rehoboam the father of Abijah, and Abijah the father of Asa.

⁸ Asa was the father of Jehoshaphat, Jehoshaphat the father of Joram, and Joram the father of Uzziah.

⁹ Uzziah was the father of Jotham, Jotham the father of Ahaz, and Ahaz the father of Hezekiah.

¹⁰ Hezekiah was the father of Manasseh, Manasseh the father of

⁵ Σαλμὼν δὲ ἐγέννησεν τὸν Βοὸζ ἐκ τῆς Ῥαχάβ· Βοὸζ δὲ ἐγέννησεν τὸν Ὠβὴδ ἐκ τῆς Ῥούθ· Ὠβὴδ δὲ ἐγέννησεν τὸν Ἰεσσαί·

⁶ Ἰεσσαὶ δὲ ἐγέννησεν τὸν Δαυὶδ τὸν βασιλέα. Δαυὶδ δὲ ὁ βασιλεὺς ἐγέννησεν τὸν Σολομῶνα ἐκ τῆς τοῦ Οὐρίου·

⁷ Σολομὼν δὲ ἐγέννησεν τὸν Ῥοβοάμ· Ῥοβοὰμ δὲ ἐγέννησεν τὸν Ἀβιά· Ἀβιὰ δὲ ἐγέννησεν τὸν Ἀσά·

⁸ Ἀσὰ δὲ ἐγέννησεν τὸν Ἰωσαφάτ· Ἰωσαφὰτ δὲ ἐγέννησεν τὸν Ἰωράμ· Ἰωρὰμ δὲ ἐγέννησεν τὸν Ὀζίαν·

⁹ Ὀζίας δὲ ἐγέννησεν τὸν Ἰωάθαμ· Ἰωάθαμ δὲ ἐγέννησεν τὸν Ἄχαζ· Ἄχαζ δὲ ἐγέννησεν τὸν Ἐζεκίαν·

¹⁰ Ἐζεκίας δὲ ἐγέννησεν τὸν Μανασσῆ· Μανασσῆς δὲ ἐγέννησεν τὸν Ἀμών·

Amon, and Amon the father of Josiah.

¹¹ Josiah became the father of Jeconiah and his brothers, at the time of the deportation to Babylon.

¹² After the deportation to Babylon: Jeconiah became the father of Shealtiel, and Shealtiel the father of Zerubbabel.

¹³ Zerubbabel was the father of Abihud, Abihud the father of Eliakim, and Eliakim the father of Azor.

¹⁴ Azor was the father of Zadok, Zadok the father of Achim, and Achim the father of Eliud.

¹⁵ Eliud was the father of Eleazar, Eleazar the father of Matthan, and Matthan the father of Jacob.

¹⁶ Jacob was the father of Joseph the husband of

Ἀμὼν δὲ ἐγέννησεν τὸν Ἰωσίαν·

¹¹ Ἰωσίας δὲ ἐγέννησεν τὸν Ἰεχονίαν καὶ τοὺς ἀδελφοὺς αὐτοῦ, ἐπὶ τῆς μετοικεσίας Βαβυλῶνος.

¹² Μετὰ δὲ τὴν μετοικεσίαν Βαβυλῶνος, Ἰεχονίας ἐγέννησεν τὸν Σαλαθιήλ· Σαλαθιὴλ δὲ ἐγέννησεν τὸν Ζοροβάβελ·

¹³ Ζοροβάβελ δὲ ἐγέννησεν τὸν Ἀβιούδ· Ἀβιοὺδ δὲ ἐγέννησεν τὸν Ἐλιακείμ· Ἐλιακεὶμ δὲ ἐγέννησεν τὸν Ἀζώρ·

¹⁴ Ἀζὼρ δὲ ἐγέννησεν τὸν Σαδώκ· Σαδὼκ δὲ ἐγέννησεν τὸν Ἀχείμ· Ἀχεὶμ δὲ ἐγέννησεν τὸν Ἐλιούδ·

¹⁵ Ἐλιοὺδ δὲ ἐγέννησεν τὸν Ἐλεάζαρ· Ἐλεάζαρ δὲ ἐγέννησεν τὸν Ματθάν· Ματθὰν δὲ ἐγέννησεν τὸν Ἰακώβ·

Mary, by whom Jesus was born, who is called the Messiah. [17] So all the generations from Abraham to David are fourteen generations; from David to the deportation to Babylon, fourteen generations; and from the deportation to Babylon to the Messiah, fourteen generations. (Matt. 1:1-17 NAU)	[16] Ἰακὼβ δὲ ἐγέννησεν τὸν Ἰωσὴφ τὸν ἄνδρα Μαρίας, ἐξ ἧς ἐγεννήθη Ἰησοῦς, ὁ λεγόμενος χριστός. [17] Πᾶσαι οὖν αἱ γενεαὶ ἀπὸ Ἀβραὰμ ἕως Δαυὶδ γενεαὶ δεκατέσσαρες· καὶ ἀπὸ Δαυὶδ ἕως τῆς μετοικεσίας Βαβυλῶνος, γενεαὶ δεκατέσσαρες· καὶ ἀπὸ τῆς μετοικεσίας Βαβυλῶνος ἕως τοῦ χριστοῦ, γενεαὶ δεκατέσσαρες. (Matt. 1:1-17 BYZ)

Process of Discovery

Linguistics Section

Linguistic Structure

[1] The record of the genealogy of Jesus the Messiah, the son of David, the son of Abraham:

[Starting With Abraham] [2] Abraham was the father of Isaac, Isaac the father of Jacob, and Jacob the father of

Judah and his brothers. ³ Judah was the father of Perez and Zerah by Tamar, Perez was the father of Hezron, and Hezron the father of Ram. ⁴ Ram was the father of Amminadab, Amminadab the father of Nahshon, and Nahshon the father of Salmon. ⁵ Salmon was the father of Boaz by Rahab, Boaz was the father of Obed by Ruth, and Obed the father of Jesse.

[David the King] ⁶ Jesse was the father of David the king. David was the father of Solomon by Bathsheba who had been the wife of Uriah. ⁷ Solomon was the father of Rehoboam, Rehoboam the father of Abijah, and Abijah the father of Asa. ⁸ Asa was the father of Jehoshaphat, Jehoshaphat the father of Joram, and Joram the father of Uzziah. ⁹ Uzziah was the father of Jotham, Jotham the father of Ahaz, and Ahaz the father of Hezekiah. ¹⁰ Hezekiah was the father of Manasseh, Manasseh the father of Amon, and Amon the father of Josiah. ¹¹ Josiah became the father of Jeconiah and his brothers, at the time of the deportation to Babylon.

[Exile to Babylon] ¹² After the deportation to Babylon: Jeconiah became the father of Shealtiel, and Shealtiel the father of Zerubbabel.¹³ Zerubbabel was the father of Abihud, Abihud the father of Eliakim, and Eliakim the father of Azor. ¹⁴ Azor was the father of Zadok, Zadok the father of Achim, and Achim the father of Eliud. ¹⁵ Eliud was the father of Eleazar,

Eleazar the father of Matthan, and Matthan the father of Jacob.

[Yeshua] [16] Jacob was the father of Joseph the husband of Mary, by whom Jesus was born, who is called the Messiah. [17] So all the generations from Abraham to David are fourteen generations; from David to the deportation to Babylon, fourteen generations; and from the deportation to Babylon to the Messiah, fourteen generations.

Discussion

The genealogy is in a simple structure showing the ancestry of Yeshua. The consensus is that this list is not necessarily an accurate list. One reason for the assessment is that 400 years separate Ram and Aminadab. The purpose of the genealogy is to set the context of the ongoing story of God's acts in history that leads to the birth of the Messiah. The names from Abraham through Zerubbabel can be reconstructed from the Septuagint; 1 Chronicles 1:28-42; 3:5-24; and Ruth 4:12-22. The names from Abiud through Jacob (verses 13-15) all occur in the

Septuagint, but not in any relation to each other.[6] Therefore, the final segment of names must have come from traditional materials which were verbally passed down through the generations.

Questioning the Passage

1. Why does the genealogy state that Yeshua is a son of David in verse one?

   The LORD chose king David to create the nation of Israel and to prepare the way for the building of the Temple. Also, the LORD promised David that a descendant of His would sit on the throne of Israel. The Davidic covenant can be found in 2 Samuel chapter seven.

2. Why does the genealogy start with Abraham?

---

[6] The New Interpreter's Bible. General Articles on the New Testament, the Gospel of Matthew, the Gospel of Mark. Nashville, TN: Abingdon, 1995.

This was done to demonstrate that Yeshua was of Jewish descent. Abraham is considered the father of the Jewish nation.

3. Why does verse two say "Judah and his brothers?"

The inclusion of the brothers could be a mechanism used by the author to show an inclusion of all peoples in the promise of the LORD through the Messiah Yeshua. The messianic tradition states that the Messiah came from the line of Judah. This could be viewed as limiting who could become a part of the Kingdom of God when the Messiah came. By including "his brothers" the author is saying that he believed that all the descendants of Jacob would be a part of the Kingdom of God. Just because Yeshua's line comes from Judah does not mean that the other tribes of Israel were not important to the LORD.

4. Why is Tamar listed in verse three?

Tamar is the first women listed in the genealogy. She was married to Er who was the first-born son of Judah. However, Er was evil in the sight of the LORD and the LORD took his life. Since Tamar did not have children it was obligation of the next oldest brother to go to Tamar and get her pregnant for his brother. This was the custom of the day. Genesis chapter thirty-eight says that Onan knew the offspring would not be considered his and he did not impregnate Tamar. Since Onan did not perform his duty for his brother the LORD took his life. At that point Judah did not want to see more of his sons die so he told Tamar to remain a widow in her father's house until Shelah, Judah's youngest son, grew up. After a considerable amount of time Tamar decided to trick Judah because she learned that Shelah was grown up and that Judah was not going to give him to her. So, she removed her widow's garments and covered herself with a veil and waited upon a road that she knew Judah would be on. Judah thought she was a common harlot and had sexual relations with her. Tamar became pregnant. Upon hearing this news Judah wanted to have her killed because he considered her an adulterous. Tamar showed Judah that she was his daughter-in-law because she had a couple of Judah's personal property from the time of their sexual encounter (payment for being a harlot). Judah called her more righteous because he did not keep up his promise to Tamar.

So, the line of Yeshua has a "bump" in the road. A promise that was made had been broken which in Judah's day was a sin before the LORD.

That sin was recognized and forgiven by the LORD because He did not kill Judah nor Tamar. The Messiah's line has forgiveness built into it from the beginning, which is a foundation of the Kingdom of God.

5. Why is Rahab listed in verse five?

Listing Rahab in the Davidic line is problematic because the timing is off. This adds to the argument that the list is not necessarily historical accurate. Having Rahab in the list is to show that Gentiles are included in the line thus, included in the promise of the Messiah Yeshua. Rahab is the women who hid the spies that Joshua sent into Jericho to gather information before the siege and invasion of the city occurred. Rahab must have loved the LORD because she risked her life for the Hebrew spies. She becomes a part of the Kingdom of God because she loved the LORD.

Loving the LORD is a foundation stone of the Kingdom of God.

6. Why is Ruth mentioned in verse five?

Ruth is important to the line because the LORD said to Israel that no Moabite was permitted to enter the assembly.

> [3] "No Ammonite or Moabite shall enter the assembly of the LORD; none of their *descendants*, even to the tenth generation, shall ever enter the assembly of the LORD, [4] because they did not meet you with food and water on the way when you came out of Egypt, and because they hired against you Balaam the son of Beor from Pethor of Mesopotamia, to curse you. (Deut. 23:3-4 NAU)

The historical timing of the genealogy can be challenged because ten generations had to pass before Moab would be permitted to intermix with Israel. Ruth was a Moabite. She was sent by her mother-in-law Naomi to seduce Boaz. He fell in love with her and made her his wife. The Gentiles are included in the line of David, which indicates that they are included in the Kingdom of God through Yeshua. In this case the Gentile enemies of Israel are included in the messianic promise. Also, the LORD decided that all nations are included in the Kingdom of God even the ones that have been cursed in the past. Forgiveness can be seen with respect to the cursed nations.

7. Why is Bathsheba mentioned in verse six?

Bathsheba was a Gentile according to rabbinic tradition because she married Uriel who was a

Gentile. Uriel was a Hittite. This could be viewed as the LORD offering forgiveness to Bathsheba for her marriage to a Gentile which was forbidden under the Torah. Again, forgiveness enters Yeshua's ancestral line.[7] Also, she is an example of a person who left the LORD then wanted to return to the LORD. The LORD wants those who became disenfranchised in His Kingdom.

8. Why does very eleven say "Jeconiah and his brothers?"

The commentators' consensus is that "his brothers" was inserted for the same reason that Judah's brothers are mentioned earlier. Jeconiah only had one brother.

9. Why is Mary mentioned in verse sixteen?

---

[7] IBID.

Mary is the mother of Yeshua and thus her mentioned in the line. The problem with the line is that Joseph, who was of the line of David, was not Yeshua's biological father. Scripture says that the Holy Spirit impregnated Mary. What is the validity of the line in Matthew's Gospel when Joseph is not the father of Yeshua? Mary's line would be the true line to be examined to determine if Yeshua was born as a son of David. In later writings, external to the Bible, this question is explored, and the answer is that Mary was from the same line as Joseph. That would make Mary and Joseph very close cousins, which would not matter if they never had sexual relations. There are places in the Scriptures and in the Yeshua tradition that Mary was a virgin and remained a virgin throughout her life. In this scenario it does not matter that Joseph and Mary were close cousins. However, there are other places in Scripture that say that Mary had other children. It was not unusual for first cousins to marry in Yeshua's day. It is possible that Joseph and Mary were cousins which would mean that Mary was born to Jacob's brother or sister (Jacob was Joseph's father).

There is a theological view that Mary was not a virgin and not impregnated by the Holy Spirit when the genealogy was put together, which would mean that Joseph was His father. The early church did not view Yeshua as God and the idea of Trinity was not developed until 325 CE. Therefore, the early church did not view Yeshua as God, which is apparent in the synoptic Gospels. The question of when Yeshua became God has been explored with differing conclusions. The Gospels that the church espouses today are not necessarily the original writing. It is well documented that changes were made to them throughout the years. Therefore, it is conceivable that the original Matthew Gospel did not have Mary as a virgin and that Yeshua was not conceived by the Holy Spirit. The tradition of Mary the virgin and Yeshua being conceived by the Holy Spirit belief may have developed years after Yeshua's life.

A possibility is that as Paul spread Christianity through the Roman world, he was converting Mithras house churches. The fast spread of Christianity would attest to this possible theory. Mithras would have been replaced by Yeshua of Nazareth. Since Mithras was born from a virgin birth by the gods, Paul would have to adopt the theology that Yeshua was a virgin birth. If he did not, then the Mithras house churches would have never evolved into the proto-orthodox churches.

The theological idea that Mary was a virgin and that Yeshua was conceived by the Holy Spirit is so strong and in many denominations of Christianity a foundational building block, that the though of it not being this way is not entertained by the theologians of the denomination. This does limit the discussion when questions arise about the way the genealogy of Yeshua is studied in Matthew's and Luke's Gospels. Therefore, the idea of Mary being a cousin of Joseph from the line of David has been adopted by Christianity.

10. What is the significance to having fourteen generations from Abraham to David and fourteen generations from David to Yeshua?

Fourteen is two times seven. Seven is a number that signifies the LORD and all His creation. The number two could be referring to the second part of the Trinity. Therefore, fourteen can be viewed as a number signifying the LORD's perfection through the second person of the Trinity, Yeshua's perfection.

Culture Section

Discussion

Semitic people considered a genealogy to be important. One of the styles of beginning a book in ancient times was to start with a genealogy. The genealogy tells us about the importance of the person whom the book is written about.

Questioning the passage

1. Is there a significance to the "son of David" title? (v. 1)

   "Son of David" is a royal and messianic title. Anyone who held this title was considered a successor of King David.

2. Were there times when the mother's name was recorded with the father's name?

   "In biblical days the Hebrews were polygamists like many other Near Eastern Semites." The mother's name would be included with the father's name when the father had several wives and the wives used the same name for their child. This would distinguish the father and the mother.

3. Mary's name is mentioned. Is this for the same reason as indicated above?

In the Peshitta (Aramaic version of the Christian Scriptures) the author used a feminine construction of the verb "beget" instead of the masculine construction, which was used throughout the preview genealogy. This was done to make it clear that Joseph's wife Mary is the one who bore Yeshua. It also indicates that Joseph had other wives.[8]

By using the Peshitta version of Matthew's Gospel the question about Mary only having one son, Yeshua, and remaining a virgin throughout her life gains validity. The brothers of Yeshua mentioned in the Gospels would have been step-brothers because Joseph's other wife/wives could have had children with Joseph.

---

[8] Errico, Rocco A., and George M. Lamsa. Aramaic Light on the Gospel of Matthew: A Commentary on the Teachings of Jesus from the Aramaic and Unchanged Near Eastern Customs. Santa Fe, NM: Noohra Foundation, 2000.

Main/Center Point

Yeshua is the descendant of King David and thus God kept His covenant with King David. The Kingdom is the Kingdom of God with Yeshua as the King. The five women demonstrate the building blocks of the kingdom of God. Each woman brings a different aspect to Christianity.

Matthew 1:1-17 – Yeshua's Genealogy

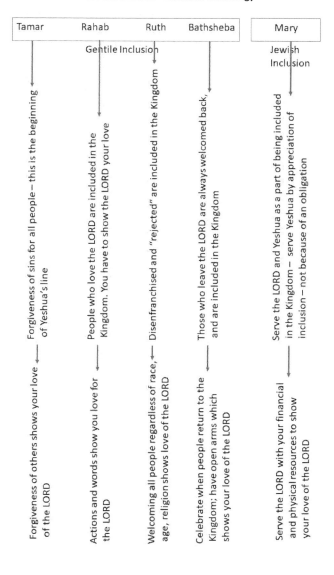

Tamar	Rahab	Ruth	Bathsheba	Mary
	Gentile Inclusion			Jewish Inclusion

Tamar: Forgiveness of sins for all people – this is the beginning of Yeshua's line

Rahab: People who love the LORD are included in the Kingdom. You have to show the LORD your love

Ruth: Disenfranchised and "rejected" are included in the Kingdom

Bathsheba: Those who leave the LORD are always welcomed back, and are included in the Kingdom

Mary: Serve the LORD and Yeshua as a part of being included in the Kingdom – serve Yeshua by appreciation of inclusion – not because of an obligation

Tamar: Forgiveness of others shows your love of the LORD

Rahab: Actions and words show you love for the LORD

Ruth: Welcoming all people regardless of race, age, religion shows love of the LORD

Bathsheba: Celebrate when people return to the Kingdom; have open arms which shows your love of the LORD

Mary: Serve the LORD with your financial and physical resources to show your love of the LORD

Thoughts

The promise of the LORD's Messiah was sent to us in the human form of Yeshua of Nazareth. The Davidic covenant states that the LORD would send a descendant of King David to rule over the Kingdom. Yeshua's kingdom was not a kingdom of humankind but rather a kingdom created by God the Father. The baby born in the manger is the King of the Kingdom of God. Yeshua's kingdom s based on spirituality making it the Kingdom of God. Also, the Messiah is of Jewish descent. The genealogy line proves without any doubt that Yeshua was Jewish, as was promised. There have been times in history where Christian theologians and leaders, like Martin Luther, who insisted that Yeshua of Nazareth was not Jewish. It is undeniable that the LORD was working through the generations until He could intervene. Yeshua is Jewish!

Reflections

In 2018 one of the big cravings is to learn about one's ancestry. There are several companies that offer DNA analysis. A good question would be, what do you do when you discover where your DNA came from? How many people are going to change something in their life because of their DNA. Many people have discovered that they are not from the area of the world that the family has always said they were from. Migrations of people throughout the centuries would explain how DNA moved from one area of the world to the another.

So, now that knowing one's ancestry is important, then this passage about Yeshua's ancestry should become important. But this passage is rarely used on a Sunday morning sermon. It should be! It is filled with so many fascinating lessons. The five women mentioned in the genealogy sets up the foundation of what the Gospel of Matthew talks about. The beginnings of the definition of the Kingdom of God is shown here. This passage should never be discounted as unimportant. God wanted the genealogy in the Gospel of Matthew, in the order and way it is presented. It should spark readers to look closer at it. So many new and exciting things can be discovered.

Works Cited

1986. *Back to School.* Directed by James Signorelli. Performed by Rodney Dangerfield.

Davis, Anne Kimball. 2012. *The Synoptic Gospels.* Albuquerque.

Errico, Rocco A., and George M. Lamsa. 2000. *Aramaic Light on the Gospel of Mattew: A Commentary on the Teachings of Jesus from the Aramaic and Unchanged Near Eastern Customs.* Santa Fe, NM: Noohra Foundation.

n.d. *Matthew Chiasm.* Accessed April 4, 2017. http://www.bible.literarystructure.info/bible/40_Matthew_pericope_e.html.

1995. *The New Interpreter's Bible Gospel of Matthew and Mark.* Nashville, TN: Abingdon Press.

Made in the USA
Monee, IL
13 January 2022